Simple 1-2-3™
One Dish

Publications International, Ltd.

Pictured on the front cover: Chicken with Rice & Asparagus Pilaf *(page 88)*.
Pictured on the back cover *(top to bottom):* Teriyaki Rib Dinner *(page 48)* and Italian-Style Sausage with Rice *(page 46)*.

ISBN-13: 978-1-60553-119-9
ISBN-10: 1-60553-119-7

Manufactured in China.

8 7 6 5 4 3 2 1

Preparation/Cooking Times: Preparation times are based on the approximate amount of time required to assemble the recipe before cooking, baking, chilling or serving. These times include preparation steps such as measuring, chopping and mixing. The fact that some preparations and cooking can be done simultaneously is taken into account. Preparation of optional ingredients and serving suggestions is not included.

Publications International, Ltd.

Contents ⋋⋌

Beef in a Hurry

Empanada Pie

- **1 pound ground beef**
- **1 small onion, chopped**
- **1 package (1¼ ounces) taco seasoning mix**
- **1 can (8 ounces) tomato sauce**
- **¼ cup raisins**
- **2 teaspoons dark brown sugar**
- **1 package (8 count) refrigerated crescent roll dough**
- **Sliced green onion (optional)**

1. Preheat oven to 375°F. Grease 10-inch shallow round baking dish or deep-dish pie plate.

2. Brown beef and onion 6 to 8 minutes over medium-high heat, stirring to break up meat. Drain fat. Sprinkle taco seasoning over beef mixture. Add tomato sauce, raisins and sugar. Reduce heat to low; cook 2 to 3 minutes.

3. Spoon beef mixture into prepared dish. Unroll crescent dough; separate into triangles. Arrange 5 triangles on top of beef mixture in a spiral with points of dough towards center (do not seal dough pieces together). Reserve remaining dough for another use. Bake 13 to 17 minutes or until dough is puffed and golden brown. Garnish with green onion.   *Makes 4 to 6 servings*

Hearty Beef and Potato Casserole

**1 package (about 17 ounces) refrigerated fully cooked
    beef pot roast in gravy***
3 cups frozen hash brown potatoes, divided
¼ teaspoon salt
¼ teaspoon black pepper
1 can (about 14 ounces) diced tomatoes
½ cup canned chipotle chile sauce
1 cup (4 ounces) shredded sharp Cheddar cheese

*Fully cooked beef pot roast can be found in the refrigerated prepared meats section of the supermarket.

1. Preheat oven to 375°F. Grease 11×7-inch glass baking dish.

2. Drain and discard gravy from pot roast. Cut beef into ¼-inch-thick slices. Place 2 cups potatoes in prepared baking dish. Sprinkle with salt and pepper. Top with beef. Combine tomatoes and chile sauce in small bowl; spread evenly over beef. Top with remaining 1 cup potatoes. Sprinkle with cheese.

3. Lightly cover dish with foil. Bake 20 minutes. Remove foil; bake 20 minutes longer or until hot and bubbly. Let stand 5 to 10 minutes before serving. *Makes 6 servings*

Tortilla Beef Casserole

1 package (about 17 ounces) refrigerated fully cooked beef pot roast in gravy*
6 (6-inch) corn tortillas, cut into 1-inch pieces
1 jar (16 ounces) salsa
1½ cups canned or thawed frozen corn
1 cup canned black or pinto beans, rinsed and drained
1 cup (4 ounces) shredded Mexican cheese blend

*Fully cooked beef pot roast can be found in the refrigerated prepared meats section of the supermarket.

1. Preheat oven to 350°F. Lightly spray 11×7-inch baking dish or 2-quart casserole with nonstick cooking spray.

2. Drain and discard gravy from pot roast. Cut or shred beef into bite-size pieces. Combine beef, tortillas, salsa, corn and beans in large bowl; mix well. Transfer to prepared dish.

3. Bake 20 minutes or until heated through. Sprinkle with cheese; bake 5 minutes or until cheese is melted. *Makes 4 servings*

Beef Teriyaki Stir-Fry

1 cup uncooked rice
1 boneless beef top sirloin steak (about 1 pound)
½ cup teriyaki sauce, divided
2 tablespoons vegetable oil, divided
1 medium onion, halved and sliced
2 cups frozen green beans, rinsed and drained

1. Cook rice according to package directions. Keep warm. Cut beef lengthwise in half, then crosswise into ⅛-inch slices. Combine beef and ¼ cup teriyaki sauce in medium bowl; set aside.

2. Heat 1½ teaspoons oil in large skillet or wok over medium-high heat. Add onion; stir-fry 3 to 4 minutes or until crisp-tender. Remove from skillet to another medium bowl. Heat 1½ teaspoons oil in skillet. Stir-fry green beans 3 minutes or until crisp-tender and heated through. Drain excess liquid. Add beans to onion in bowl.

3. Heat remaining 1 tablespoon oil in skillet. Drain beef, discarding marinade. Stir-fry half of beef 2 minutes or until barely pink in center. Add to vegetables. Repeat with remaining beef. Return beef mixture to skillet. Stir in remaining ¼ cup teriyaki sauce; cook and stir 1 minute or until heated through. Serve with rice. *Makes 4 servings*

Prep and Cook Time: 22 minutes

Southwestern Enchiladas

1 can (10 ounces) enchilada sauce, divided
**2 packages (about 6 ounces each) refrigerated fully cooked seasoned
steak strips***
4 (8-inch) flour tortillas
**½ cup condensed nacho cheese soup, undiluted or chile-flavored
pasteurized process cheese spread**
1½ cups (6 ounces) shredded Mexican cheese blend

**Fully cooked steak strips can be found in the refrigerated prepared meats section of the
supermarket.*

1. Preheat oven to 350°F. Spread half of enchilada sauce in 9-inch square
glass baking dish.

2. Arrange one fourth of steak down center of each tortilla. Top evenly
with cheese soup. Roll up tortillas; place seam side down in baking dish.

3. Pour remaining enchilada sauce evenly over tortillas. Sprinkle with
cheese blend. Bake 20 to 25 minutes or until heated through.

Makes 4 servings

Meatballs in Burgundy Sauce

60 frozen fully cooked meatballs, partially thawed and separated
3 cups chopped onions
1½ cups water
1 cup red wine
¼ cup ketchup
2 packages (about 1 ounce each) beef gravy mix
1 tablespoon dried oregano
1 package (8 ounces) egg noodles

SLOW COOKER DIRECTIONS

1. Combine meatballs, onions, water, wine, ketchup, gravy mix and oregano in slow cooker; stir to blend.

2. Cover; cook on HIGH 4 to 5 hours.

3. Meanwhile, cook noodles according to package directions. Serve meatballs over noodles. *Makes 6 to 8 servings*

Mexican Lasagna

**1 jar (1 pound 10 ounces) RAGÚ® Old World Style® Pasta Sauce
1 pound ground beef
1 can (15¼ ounces) whole kernel corn, drained
4½ teaspoons chili powder
6 (8½-inch) flour tortillas
2 cups shredded Cheddar cheese (about 8 ounces)**

1. Preheat oven to 350°F. Set aside 1 cup Ragú Pasta Sauce. In 10-inch skillet, brown ground beef over medium-high heat; drain. Stir in remaining Ragú Pasta Sauce, corn and chili powder.

2. In 13×9-inch baking dish, spread 1 cup sauce mixture. Arrange two tortillas over sauce, overlapping edges slightly. Layer half the sauce mixture and ⅓ of the cheese over tortillas; repeat layers, ending with tortillas. Spread tortillas with reserved sauce.

3. Bake 30 minutes, then top with remaining cheese and bake an additional 10 minutes or until sauce is bubbling and cheese is melted.

Makes 8 servings

Prep Time: 10 minutes • Cook Time: 40 minutes

Hearty Shepherd's Pie

1½ **pounds ground beef**
2 **cups** *French's*® **French Fried Onions**
1 **can (10¾ ounces) condensed tomato soup**
½ **cup water**
2 **teaspoons Italian seasoning**
¼ **teaspoon salt**
¼ **teaspoon black pepper**
1 **package (10 ounces) frozen mixed vegetables, thawed**
3 **cups hot mashed potatoes**

1. Preheat oven to 375°F. Cook meat in large ovenproof skillet until browned; drain. Stir in *1 cup* French Fried Onions, soup, water, seasoning, salt and pepper.

2. Spoon vegetables over beef mixture. Top with mashed potatoes.

3. Bake 20 minutes or until hot. Sprinkle with remaining *1 cup* onions. Bake 2 minutes or until golden.   *Makes 6 servings*

Prep Time: 10 minutes • Cook Time: 27 minutes

Spaghetti Rolls

**1 package (8 ounces) manicotti
    shells
2 pounds ground beef
1 tablespoon onion powder
1 teaspoon salt
½ teaspoon black pepper
2 cups pasta sauce, divided
1 cup (4 ounces) shredded
    mozzarella cheese or pizza
    cheese blend**

1. Cook pasta according to package
directions. Drain in colander, then
rinse under warm running water.
Drain well.

2. Meanwhile, preheat oven to
350°F. Grease 13×9-inch baking
pan. Brown beef in large skillet 6 to
8 minutes over medium-high heat, stirring to break up meat. Drain fat.
Stir in onion powder, salt and pepper. Stir in 1 cup pasta sauce. Reserve
½ cup ground beef mixture.

3. Combine remaining beef mixture with cheese in large bowl. Fill shells
with beef mixture; arrange in prepared pan. Combine remaining 1 cup
pasta sauce and reserved beef mixture in small bowl; stir well. Pour over
shells. Cover with foil. Bake 20 to 30 minutes or until heated through.

Makes 4 servings

Mushroom-Beef Stew

1 pound beef stew meat
1 can (10¾ ounces) condensed
    cream of mushroom soup,
    undiluted
2 cans (4 ounces each) sliced
    mushrooms, drained
1 package (1 ounce) dry onion
    soup mix
Hot cooked noodles
Minced fresh basil (optional)
Chopped red bell pepper
    (optional)

SLOW COOKER DIRECTIONS

1. Combine beef, condensed soup, mushrooms and soup mix in slow cooker. Cover; cook on LOW 8 to 10 hours.

2. Serve over noodles. Garnish with basil and bell pepper.

Makes 4 servings

Pizza Pie Meatloaf

  2 pounds ground beef
1½ cups shredded mozzarella cheese, divided
  ½ cup unseasoned dry bread crumbs
  1 cup tomato sauce, divided
  ¼ cup grated Parmesan cheese
  ¼ cup *French's*® Worcestershire Sauce
  1 tablespoon dried oregano leaves
  1 plum tomato, thinly sliced
  ½ cup sliced green bell pepper
1⅓ cups *French's*® French Fried Onions

1. Preheat oven to 350°F. Combine beef, *½ cup* mozzarella cheese, bread crumbs, *½ cup* tomato sauce, Parmesan cheese, Worcestershire and oregano in large bowl; stir with fork until well blended.

2. Place meat mixture into round pizza pan with edge or pie plate and shape into 9×1-inch round. Bake 35 minutes or until no longer pink in center and internal temperature reads 160°F. Drain fat.

3. Top with remaining tomato sauce, sliced tomato, green bell pepper strips, mozzarella cheese and French Fried Onions. Bake 5 minutes or until cheese is melted and onions are golden. Cut into wedges to serve.

Makes 6 to 8 servings

Prep Time: 10 minutes • Cook Time: 40 minutes

Mexican-Style Shredded Beef

1 boneless beef chuck shoulder roast (about 3 pounds)
1 tablespoon ground cumin
1 tablespoon ground coriander
1 tablespoon chili powder
1 teaspoon salt
½ teaspoon ground red pepper
1 cup salsa or picante sauce
2 tablespoons water
1 tablespoon cornstarch
Taco shells and/or flour or corn tortillas

SLOW COOKER DIRECTIONS

1. Cut roast in half. Combine cumin, coriander, chili powder, salt and red pepper in small bowl. Rub over roast. Place ¼ cup salsa in slow cooker; top with one piece of beef. Layer ¼ cup salsa, remaining beef and ½ cup salsa in slow cooker. Cover; cook on LOW 8 to 10 hours.

2. Remove roast from cooking liquid; cool slightly. Trim and discard fat. Shred meat with two forks. Let cooking liquid stand 5 minutes to allow fat to rise. Skim off fat. *Increase heat to high.* Blend water and cornstarch in small bowl until smooth. Whisk into liquid in slow cooker. Cook, uncovered, 15 minutes or until thickened.

3. Return beef to slow cooker. Cover; cook 15 minutes or until heated through. Adjust seasonings. Serve in taco shells. Leftover beef may be refrigerated up to 3 days or frozen up to 3 months.

Makes 4 to 6 servings

Prep Time: 12 minutes • Cook Time: 8½ to 10½ hours

Biscuit-Topped Hearty Steak Pie

**1½ pounds top round steak, cooked and cut into 1-inch cubes
1 package (9 ounces) frozen baby carrots
1 package (9 ounces) frozen peas and pearl onions
1 large baking potato, baked and cut into ½-inch pieces
1 jar (18 ounces) home-style brown gravy
½ teaspoon dried thyme
½ teaspoon black pepper
1 can (10 ounces) refrigerated flaky buttermilk biscuit dough**

1. Preheat oven to 375°F. Spray 2-quart casserole with nonstick cooking spray.

2. Combine steak, frozen vegetables and potato in prepared dish. Stir in gravy, thyme and pepper.

3. Bake, uncovered, 40 minutes. Remove from oven. *Increase oven temperature to 400°F.* Top with biscuits and bake 8 to 10 minutes or until biscuits are golden brown.   *Makes 6 servings*

Variations: This casserole can be prepared with leftovers of almost any kind. Other steaks, roast beef, stew meat, pork, lamb or chicken can be substituted for the round steak. Adjust the gravy flavor to complement the meat. Red potatoes can be used in place of the baking potato. Choose your favorite vegetable combination, such as broccoli, cauliflower and carrots, or broccoli, corn and red peppers, as a substitute for the carrots, peas and onions.

Easy Family Burritos

1 boneless beef chuck shoulder roast (2 to 3 pounds)
1 jar (24 ounces) or 2 jars (16 ounces each) salsa
 Flour tortillas, warmed
 Shredded Cheddar cheese, sour cream, salsa, lettuce, tomato, onion
  and/or guacamole (optional)

SLOW COOKER DIRECTIONS

1. Place roast in slow cooker; top with salsa. Cover; cook on LOW 8 to 10 hours.

2. Remove beef from slow cooker. Shred beef with 2 forks. Return to slow cooker. Cover; cook 1 to 2 hours or until heated through.

3. Serve shredded beef wrapped in warm tortillas with desired toppings.

Makes 8 servings

Tip: Make a batch of burrito meat and freeze it in family-size portions. It's quick and easy to reheat in the microwave on busy nights when there's no time to cook.

Tamale Beef Squares

 1 package (about 6 ounces) corn muffin or corn bread mix
 ⅓ cup milk
 1 egg
 1 tablespoon canola oil
 1 pound ground beef
 ¾ cup chopped onion
 1 cup frozen corn
 1 can (about 14 ounces) Mexican-style stewed tomatoes
 2 teaspoons cornstarch
 ¾ cup (3 ounces) shredded Cheddar cheese

1. Preheat oven to 400°F. Spray 12×8-inch baking dish with nonstick cooking spray. Stir together corn muffin mix, milk, egg and oil in medium bowl. Spread in prepared dish.

2. Brown ground beef and onion in large skillet 6 to 8 minutes over medium-high heat, stirring to break up meat. Drain fat. Stir in corn. Stir tomatoes and cornstarch in medium bowl, breaking up any large pieces of tomato. Stir into beef mixture in skillet. Bring to a boil, stirring frequently.

3. Spoon beef mixture over corn muffin mixture in baking dish. Cover with foil; bake 15 minutes. Remove foil; bake 10 minutes more. Sprinkle with cheese. Bake 2 to 3 minutes or until cheese is melted. Remove from oven; let stand 5 minutes. Cut into squares.   *Makes 6 servings*

Stir-Fry Beef & Vegetable Soup

1 boneless beef top sirloin or top round steak (about 1 pound)
2 teaspoons dark sesame oil, divided
3 cans (about 14 ounces each) beef broth
1 package (16 ounces) frozen stir-fry vegetables
3 green onions, thinly sliced
¼ cup stir-fry sauce
 Sesame seeds (optional)

1. Slice beef lengthwise in half, then crosswise into ⅛-inch-thick strips.

2. Heat 1 teaspoon sesame oil in large saucepan or Dutch oven over medium-high heat; tilt pan to coat bottom. Add half of beef in single layer. Cook 1 minute, without stirring, until lightly browned on bottom. Turn and cook other side about 1 minute. Remove beef from pan. Repeat with remaining 1 teaspoon sesame oil and beef; set aside.

3. Add broth to saucepan. Cover; bring to a boil over high heat. Add vegetables. Reduce heat; simmer 3 to 5 minutes or until vegetables are heated through. Add beef, green onions and stir-fry sauce; simmer 1 minute. Garnish with sesame seeds.   *Makes 6 servings*

Serving Suggestion: Make a quick sesame bread to serve with this soup. Brush refrigerated dinner roll dough with water, then dip in sesame seeds before baking.

Prep and Cook Time: 22 minutes

Cajun Chili

1½ pounds ground beef
2 cans (15 ounces each) Cajun-style mixed vegetables, undrained
2 cans (10¾ ounces each) condensed tomato soup, undiluted
1 can (about 14 ounces) diced tomatoes
3 sausages with Cheddar cheese (about 8 ounces), cut into bite-size pieces
Shredded Cheddar cheese (optional)

SLOW COOKER DIRECTIONS

1. Brown beef 6 to 8 minutes in large skillet over medium-high heat, stirring to break up meat. Drain fat.

2. Place beef, mixed vegetables with juice, soup, tomatoes and sausages in slow cooker.

3. Cover; cook on HIGH 2 to 3 hours. Top with cheese.

Makes 10 servings

Tamale Pie

1 tablespoon BERTOLLI® Olive Oil
1 small onion, chopped
1 pound ground beef
1 envelope LIPTON® RECIPE SECRETS® Onion Soup Mix*
1 can (14½ ounces) stewed tomatoes, undrained
½ cup water
1 can (15 to 19 ounces) red kidney beans, rinsed and drained
1 package (8½ ounces) corn muffin mix, plus ingredients to prepare mix

*Also terrific with LIPTON® RECIPE SECRETS® Onion Mushroom or Beefy Onion Soup Mix.

1. Preheat oven to 400°F.

2. In 12-inch skillet, heat olive oil over medium heat and cook onion, stirring occasionally, 3 minutes or until tender. Stir in ground beef and cook until browned.

3. Stir in soup mix blended with tomatoes and water. Bring to a boil over high heat, stirring with spoon to crush tomatoes. Reduce heat to low and stir in beans. Simmer, uncovered, stirring occasionally, 10 minutes. Turn into 2-quart casserole.

4. Prepare corn muffin mix according to package directions. Spoon evenly over casserole.

5. Bake, uncovered, 15 minutes or until corn topping is golden and filling is hot.   *Makes 6 servings*

Oven-Baked Stew

2 pounds boneless beef chuck or round steak, cut into 1-inch cubes
¼ cup all-purpose flour
1⅓ cups sliced carrots
1 can (14 to 16 ounces) whole peeled tomatoes, undrained and chopped
1 envelope LIPTON® RECIPE SECRETS® Onion Soup Mix*
½ cup dry red wine or water
1 cup fresh or canned sliced mushrooms
1 package (8 ounces) medium or broad egg noodles, cooked and drained

*Also terrific with LIPTON® RECIPE SECRETS® Beefy Onion or Onion Mushroom Soup Mix.

1. Preheat oven to 425°F. In 2½-quart shallow casserole, toss beef with flour, then bake, uncovered, 20 minutes, stirring once.

2. Reduce heat to 350°F. Stir in carrots, tomatoes, soup mix and wine.

3. Bake, covered, 1½ hours or until beef is tender. Stir in mushrooms and bake, covered, an additional 10 minutes. Serve over hot noodles.

Makes 8 servings

Slow Cooker Method: In slow cooker, toss beef with flour. Add carrots, tomatoes, soup mix and wine. Cook, covered, on LOW 8 to 10 hours. Add mushrooms; cook, covered, on LOW 30 minutes or until beef is tender. Serve over hot noodles.

Prep Time: 20 minutes • Cook Time: 2 hours

Beef and Broccoli

1 pound beef tenderloin steaks
2 teaspoons minced fresh ginger
2 cloves garlic, minced
½ teaspoon vegetable oil
3 cups broccoli florets
¼ cup water
2 tablespoons teriyaki sauce
2 cups hot cooked rice

1. Cut beef crosswise into ⅛-inch-thick slices. Toss beef with ginger and garlic in medium bowl.

2. Heat oil in large nonstick skillet or wok over medium heat. Add half of beef mixture; stir-fry 2 to 3 minutes or until beef is barely pink in center. Remove from skillet to medium bowl. Repeat with remaining beef.

3. Place broccoli and water in skillet; cover and steam 3 to 5 minutes or until broccoli is crisp-tender. Return beef and any accumulated juices to skillet. Add teriyaki sauce; cook until heated through. Serve over rice.

Makes 4 servings

Rush-Hour Pork

Southern Pork Barbecue Dinner

   1 tablespoon vegetable oil
½ cup chopped onion
½ cup chopped celery
½ cup chopped green bell pepper
   1 container (about 18 ounces) refrigerated fully cooked shredded pork
   1 can (about 15 ounces) pinto beans or black-eyed peas, rinsed and drained
   1 can (8 ounces) tomato sauce
   2 tablespoons Dijon mustard

1. Heat oil in large skillet over medium-high heat. Add onion, celery and bell pepper; cook and stir 5 minutes or until tender.

2. Stir in pork, beans, tomato sauce and mustard.

3. Cook over low heat 5 to 10 minutes or until heated through.

Makes 4 to 6 servings

Variation: To make sandwiches, omit the beans and serve the barbecued pork on buns.

Hearty Pork, Apple and Noodle Skillet

2 apples, such as Fuji, Gala or Golden Delicious, peeled and cored
2 tablespoons butter, divided
1 small onion, finely chopped
1 package (about 27 ounces) garlic and herb marinated pork loin fillet
1½ cups chicken broth
½ cup milk
1 package (about 4 ounces) stroganoff pasta mix
¼ teaspoon black pepper
¼ cup sour cream

1. Cut apples into ¼-inch-thick slices. Melt 1 tablespoon butter in large nonstick skillet over medium heat. Add apples and onion. Cook 5 to 10 minutes or until apples are lightly browned. Remove to small bowl; set aside.

2. Cut half of pork loin into ½-inch-thick slices. (Reserve remaining pork for another meal.) Melt remaining 1 tablespoon butter in skillet over medium heat. Brown pork in 2 batches, 2 to 3 minutes per side. *Do not overcook*. Remove to platter; keep warm.

3. Place broth and milk in skillet; bring to a boil. Add pasta mix, apple mixture and pepper; mix well. Cook over medium heat 10 minutes or until noodles are tender and sauce is slightly thickened. Stir in sour cream. Serve with pork. *Make 4 servings*

Italian-Style Sausage with Rice

1 pound mild Italian sausage links, cut into 1-inch pieces
1 can (about 15 ounces) pinto beans, rinsed and drained
1 cup pasta sauce
1 green bell pepper, cut into strips
1 small onion, halved and sliced
½ teaspoon salt
¼ teaspoon black pepper
   Hot cooked rice
   Fresh basil (optional)

SLOW COOKER DIRECTIONS

1. Cook sausage in large nonstick skillet over medium-high heat, stirring to break up meat, until cooked through. Drain fat.

2. Place sausage, beans, pasta sauce, bell pepper, onion, salt and black pepper in slow cooker. Cover; cook on LOW 4 to 6 hours.

3. Serve with rice. Garnish with basil.   *Makes 4 to 5 servings*

Prep Time: 10 to 15 minutes • Cook Time: 4 to 6 hours (LOW)

Teriyaki Rib Dinner

1 package (about 15 ounces) refrigerated fully cooked pork back ribs in barbecue sauce
2 tablespoons vegetable oil
1 large onion, thinly sliced
4 cups frozen Japanese-style stir-fry vegetables
1 can (8 ounces) pineapple chunks, undrained *or* 1 cup diced fresh pineapple
¼ cup hoisin sauce
2 tablespoons cider vinegar

1. Remove ribs from package; reserve remaining barbecue sauce. Cut into individual ribs; set aside.

2. Heat oil in Dutch oven over medium-high heat. Add onion; cook 3 minutes or until translucent. Add vegetables; cook and stir 4 minutes.

3. Add ribs, reserved sauce, pineapple with juice, hoisin sauce and vinegar to vegetable mixture; mix well. Cover; cook 5 minutes or until heated through.   *Makes 4 servings*

Harvest Ham Supper

6 carrots, cut into 2-inch pieces
3 medium sweet potatoes, quartered
1 to 1½ pounds boneless ham
1 cup maple syrup

SLOW COOKER DIRECTIONS

1. Place carrots and potatoes in bottom of slow cooker. Place ham on top of vegetables. Pour syrup over ham and vegetables.

2. Cover; cook on LOW 6 to 8 hours.   *Makes 6 servings*

Prep Time: 10 minutes • Cook Time: 6 to 8 hours (LOW)

Serving Suggestion: This dish is great served with cornbread.

Sausage and Broccoli Noodle Casserole

1 jar (1 pound) RAGÚ® Cheesy! Classic Alfredo Sauce
⅓ cup milk
1 pound sweet Italian sausage, cooked and crumbled
1 package (9 ounces) frozen chopped broccoli, thawed
8 ounces egg noodles, cooked and drained
1 cup shredded Cheddar cheese (about 4 ounces), divided
¼ cup chopped roasted red peppers

1. Preheat oven to 350°F. In large bowl, combine Alfredo Sauce and milk. Stir in sausage, broccoli, noodles, ¾ cup cheese and roasted peppers.

2. In 13×9-inch baking dish, evenly spread sausage mixture. Sprinkle with remaining ¼ cup cheese.

3. Bake 30 minutes or until heated through. *Makes 6 servings*

Prep Time: 15 minutes • Cook Time: 30 minutes

Pork with Savory Apple Stuffing

1 package (6 ounces) corn bread stuffing mix
1 can (14½ ounces) chicken broth
1 small apple, peeled, cored and chopped
¼ cup chopped celery
1⅓ cups *French's*® French Fried Onions, divided
4 boneless pork chops, ¾ inch thick (about 1 pound)
½ cup peach-apricot sweet & sour sauce
1 tablespoon *French's*® Honey Dijon Mustard

1. Preheat oven to 375°F. Combine stuffing mix, broth, apple, celery and ⅔ *cup* French Fried Onions in large bowl. Spoon into bottom of greased shallow 2-quart baking dish. Arrange chops on top of stuffing.

2. Combine sweet & sour sauce with mustard in small bowl. Pour over pork. Bake 40 minutes or until pork is no longer pink in center.

3. Sprinkle with remaining onions. Bake 5 minutes or until onions are golden.   *Makes 4 servings*

Prep Time: 10 minutes • Cook Time: 45 minutes

Creamy Ham and Garden Rotini

8 ounces uncooked rotini pasta
1 bag (16 ounces) frozen vegetable blend (broccoli, cauliflower,
    red peppers and corn)
4 ounces ham, chopped
1½ cups milk
2 tablespoons all-purpose flour
1¼ cups (5 ounces) shredded Monterey Jack cheese
    Black pepper

1. Preheat oven to 325°F. Spray 11×8-inch baking pan with nonstick cooking spray. Cook pasta according to package directions; drain. Spread in prepared pan; set aside.

2. Meanwhile, pour ½ cup water into large nonstick skillet. Bring to a boil over high heat. Add vegetables; return to a boil. Reduce heat to low. Simmer, covered, 4 minutes. Drain. Toss vegetables and ham with pasta; set aside.

3. Whisk milk and flour in small bowl until smooth. Pour milk mixture into same skillet; cook over medium-high heat, stirring constantly, until slightly thickened. Pour over pasta mixture. Top with cheese; sprinkle with black pepper. Cover loosely with foil. Bake 25 to 30 minutes or until heated through. *Makes 4 servings*

Fiesta Rice and Sausage

2 pounds spicy Italian sausage, casings removed
2 cloves garlic, minced
2 teaspoons ground cumin
4 onions, chopped
4 green bell peppers, chopped
3 jalapeño peppers,* seeded and minced
4 cups beef broth
2 packages (6¼ ounces each) long grain and wild rice mix

*Jalapeño peppers can sting and irritate the skin, so wear rubber gloves when handling peppers and do not touch your eyes.

SLOW COOKER DIRECTIONS

1. Cook sausage in large nonstick skillet over medium-high heat, stirring to break up meat, until cooked through. Drain fat. Add garlic and cumin; cook and stir 30 seconds. Add onions, bell peppers and jalapeño peppers. Cook and stir 5 minutes or until onions are tender.

2. Transfer mixture to slow cooker. Stir in broth and rice.

3. Cover; cook on LOW 4 to 6 hours or on HIGH 2 to 3 hours.

Makes 10 to 12 servings

Bacon & Potato Frittata

2 cups frozen O'Brien hash brown potatoes with onions and peppers
3 tablespoons butter
5 eggs
½ cup cooked, crumbled bacon
¼ cup half-and-half or milk
⅛ teaspoon salt
⅛ teaspoon black pepper

1. Preheat broiler. Place potatoes in medium microwavable bowl; microwave on HIGH 1 minute. Melt butter in large ovenproof skillet over medium-high heat. Swirl butter up side of pan to prevent eggs from sticking. Add potatoes; cook 3 minutes, stirring occasionally.

2. Beat eggs in medium bowl. Add bacon, half-and-half, salt and pepper; mix well. Stir egg mixture into skillet; reduce heat to medium. Cover and cook 6 minutes or until eggs are set at edges (top will still be wet).

3. Transfer skillet to broiler. Broil 4 inches from heat 1 to 2 minutes or until center is set and frittata is golden brown. Cut into wedges.

Makes 4 servings

Serving Suggestion: Top frittata with red bell pepper strips, chopped chives and salsa.

Prep and Cook Time: 20 minutes

Skillet Sausage and Bean Stew

    1 pound spicy Italian sausage, cut into pieces
½ onion, chopped
    2 cups frozen O'Brien hash brown potatoes with onions and peppers
    1 can (about 15 ounces) pinto beans, undrained
¾ cup water
    1 teaspoon beef bouillon granules *or* 1 beef bouillon cube
    1 teaspoon dried oregano
⅛ teaspoon ground red pepper

1. Cook sausage and onion in large skillet over medium-high heat, stirring to break up meat, until sausage is cooked through. Drain fat.

2. Stir in potatoes, beans, water, bouillon, oregano and red pepper; reduce heat to medium. Cover; simmer 15 minutes, stirring occasionally.

Makes 4 servings

Prep and Cook Time: 30 minutes

Italian-Glazed Pork Chops

1 tablespoon olive oil
8 bone-in pork chops
1 medium zucchini, thinly sliced
1 medium red bell pepper, chopped
1 medium onion, thinly sliced
3 cloves garlic, finely chopped
¼ cup dry red wine or beef broth
1 jar (1 pound 10 ounces) RAGÚ® Chunky Pasta Sauce

1. In 12-inch skillet, heat olive oil over medium-high heat and brown chops. Remove chops and set aside.

2. In same skillet, cook zucchini, red bell pepper, onion and garlic, stirring occasionally, 4 minutes. Stir in wine and Ragú Pasta Sauce.

3. Return chops to skillet, turning to coat with sauce. Simmer, covered, 15 minutes or until chops are tender and barely pink in the center. Serve, if desired, over hot cooked couscous or rice.   *Makes 8 servings*

Prep Time: 10 minutes • Cook Time: 25 minutes

Sweet and Savory Sausage Casserole

2 sweet potatoes, peeled and cut into 1-inch cubes
2 apples, peeled, cored and cut into 1-inch cubes
1 medium onion, cut into thin strips
2 tablespoons vegetable oil
2 teaspoons Italian seasoning
1 teaspoon garlic powder
½ teaspoon salt
½ teaspoon black pepper
1 pound cooked Italian sausage, cut into ½-inch pieces

1. Preheat oven to 400°F. Spray 13×9-inch baking pan with nonstick cooking spray.

2. Combine potatoes, apples, onion, oil, Italian seasoning, garlic powder, salt and pepper in large bowl. Toss to coat evenly. Place potato mixture in prepared pan.

3. Bake, covered, 30 minutes. Add sausage to potato mixture; bake 5 to 10 minutes or until sausage is heated through and potatoes are tender.

Makes 4 to 6 servings

Hearty Noodle Casserole

1 pound Italian sausage, casings removed
1 jar (26½ ounces) pasta sauce
2 cups (16 ounces) ricotta or cottage cheese
1 package (12 ounces) extra wide egg noodles, cooked and drained
2 cups (8 ounces) shredded mozzarella cheese, divided
1 can (4 ounces) sliced mushrooms
½ cup chopped green bell pepper
    Chopped fresh basil (optional)

1. Preheat oven to 350°F. Cook sausage in large skillet over medium-high heat, stirring to break up meat, until cooked through. Drain fat.

2. Combine sausage, sauce, ricotta cheese, noodles, half of mozzarella cheese, mushrooms and bell pepper in large bowl. Spoon into 3-quart or 13×9-inch baking pan. Top with remaining mozzarella cheese.

3. Bake, uncovered, about 25 minutes or until heated through. Garnish with basil.

Makes 4 to 6 servings

Carolina Baked Beans & Pork Chops

2 cans (16 ounces each) pork and beans
½ cup chopped onion
½ cup chopped green bell pepper
¼ cup *French's® Classic Yellow®* Mustard
¼ cup packed light brown sugar
2 tablespoons *French's®* Worcestershire Sauce
1 tablespoon *Frank's® RedHot®* Original Cayenne Pepper Sauce
6 boneless pork chops (1 inch thick)

1. Preheat oven to 400°F. Combine all ingredients *except pork chops* in 3-quart shallow baking dish; mix well. Arrange chops on top, turning once to coat with sauce.

2. Bake, uncovered, 30 to 35 minutes or until pork is no longer pink in center. Stir beans around chops once during baking. Serve with green beans or mashed potatoes, if desired.   *Makes 6 servings*

Prep Time: 10 minutes • Cook Time: 30 minutes

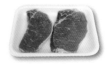

Tuscan Pot Pie

¾ pound sweet or hot Italian sausage
1 jar (26 to 28 ounces) chunky vegetable or mushroom spaghetti sauce
1 can (19 ounces) cannellini beans, rinsed and drained
½ teaspoon dried thyme
1½ cups (6 ounces) shredded mozzarella cheese
1 package (8 ounces) refrigerated crescent roll dough

1. Preheat oven to 425°F. Remove sausage from casings.* Cook sausage in medium ovenproof skillet, stirring to break up meat, until cooked through. Drain fat.

2. Add spaghetti sauce, beans and thyme to skillet. Simmer, uncovered, over medium heat 5 minutes. Remove from heat; stir in cheese.

3. Unroll crescent dough; divide into triangles. Arrange in spiral with points of dough toward center, covering sausage mixture completely. Bake 12 minutes or until crust is golden brown and meat mixture is hot and bubbly.   *Makes 4 to 6 servings*

*To remove a sausage casing, use a paring knife to slit the casing at one end. Be careful not to cut through the sausage. Grasp the cut edge and gently pull the casing away.

Prep and Cook Time: 27 minutes

Polish Reuben Casserole

2 cans (10¾ ounces each) condensed cream of mushroom soup, undiluted
1⅓ cups milk
½ cup chopped onion
1 tablespoon prepared mustard
1 jar (32 ounces) sauerkraut, rinsed and drained
1 package (8 ounces) uncooked medium egg noodles
1½ pounds Polish sausage, cut into ½-inch pieces
2 cups (8 ounces) shredded Swiss cheese
¾ cup whole wheat bread crumbs
2 tablespoons butter, melted

1. Preheat oven to 350°F. Grease 13×9-inch baking dish. Combine soup, milk, onion and mustard in medium bowl; stir well.

2. Spread sauerkraut in prepared dish. Top with noodles. Spoon soup mixture evenly over noodles; cover with sausage. Top with cheese.

3. Combine bread crumbs and butter in small bowl; sprinkle over casserole. Cover dish tightly with foil. Bake about 1 hour or until noodles are tender. *Makes 8 to 10 servings*

No-Hassle Poultry

Southwestern Turkey Stew

1 tablespoon vegetable oil
1 small onion, finely chopped
1 clove garlic, minced
2 cups chicken broth
2 cups cooked smoked turkey breast, cut into ½-inch pieces
2 cups frozen corn
1 can (about 14 ounces) diced tomatoes
1 package (about 6 ounces) red beans and rice mix
1 to 2 canned chipotle peppers in adobo sauce,* drained and minced
   Chopped green onion (optional)

Canned chipotle peppers can be found in the Mexican section of most supermarkets.

1. Heat oil in large skillet over medium-high heat. Add onion and garlic; cook and stir 3 minutes or until onion is translucent.

2. Add broth; bring to a boil. Stir in turkey, corn, tomatoes, rice mix and chipotle pepper. Reduce heat to low.

3. Cover; cook 10 to 12 minutes or until rice is tender. Let stand 3 minutes. Garnish with green onion. *Makes 4 servings*

Variations: Use 1 can (about 14 ounces) diced tomatoes with jalapeño peppers in place of the diced tomatoes. Or use ¼ teaspoon chipotle chili powder and 1 minced jalapeño pepper in place of the chipotle peppers.

Easy Cajun Chicken Stew

- **2 tablespoons vegetable oil**
- **1 red bell pepper, diced**
- **1 stalk celery, sliced**
- **1 can (about 14 ounces) diced tomatoes with roasted garlic and onions**
- **1½ cups chicken broth**
- **1 package (about 10 ounces) refrigerated fully cooked chicken breast strips, cut into pieces**
- **1 pouch (about 9 ounces) New Orleans-style chicken-flavored ready-to-serve rice mix**
- **1 cup canned kidney beans, rinsed and drained**
- **¼ teaspoon hot pepper sauce**
- **¼ cup chopped green onions**

1. Heat oil in large saucepan or Dutch oven over medium-high heat. Add bell pepper and celery; cook and stir 3 minutes. Add tomatoes and broth; bring to a boil.

2. Add chicken, rice mix, beans and pepper sauce. Reduce heat to low. Cover; cook 7 minutes.

3. Stir in green onions. Remove from heat. Cover; let stand 2 to 3 minutes to thicken.   *Makes 4 servings*

Variation: If canned diced tomatoes with garlic and onions are not available, substitute 1 can (about 14 ounces) diced tomatoes, ¼ cup chopped onion and 1 teaspoon minced garlic.

Broccoli, Turkey and Noodle Skillet

1 tablespoon butter
1 green bell pepper, chopped
1 cup frozen chopped broccoli, thawed
¼ teaspoon black pepper
1½ cups chicken broth
½ cup milk or half-and-half
2 cups diced cooked turkey breast
1 package (about 4 ounces) chicken and broccoli pasta mix
¼ cup sour cream

1. Melt butter in large skillet over medium-high heat. Add bell pepper, broccoli and black pepper; cook and stir 5 minutes or until bell pepper is crisp-tender.

2. Add broth and milk; bring to a boil. Stir in turkey and pasta mix. Reduce heat to low. Cook 8 to 10 minutes or until noodles are tender. Remove from heat.

3. Stir in sour cream. Let stand, uncovered, 5 minutes or until sauce thickens.   *Makes 4 servings*

Quick Hot and Sour Chicken Soup

2 cups water
2 cups chicken broth
1 package (about 10 ounces) refrigerated fully cooked chicken breast
   strips, cut into pieces
1 package (about 7 ounces) chicken-flavored rice and vermicelli mix
1 jalapeño pepper,* minced
2 green onions, chopped
1 tablespoon soy sauce
1 tablespoon lime juice
1 tablespoon minced fresh cilantro

*Jalapeño peppers can sting and irritate the skin, so wear rubber gloves when handling peppers and do not touch your eyes.

1. Combine water, broth, chicken, rice mix, jalapeño pepper, green onions and soy sauce in large saucepan; bring to a boil over high heat.

2. Reduce heat to low. Cover; simmer 20 minutes or until rice is tender, stirring occasionally.

3. Stir in lime juice and sprinkle with cilantro.   *Makes 4 servings*

30-Minute Paella

2 tablespoons olive oil
1 package (about 10 ounces) chicken-flavored rice and vermicelli mix
¼ teaspoon red pepper flakes
3½ cups water
1 package (about 10 ounces) refrigerated fully cooked chicken breast strips, cut into ½-inch pieces
1 package (8 ounces) medium raw shrimp, peeled
1 cup frozen peas
¼ cup diced roasted red pepper

1. Heat oil in large skillet over medium heat. Add vermicelli mix and red pepper flakes; cook and stir 2 minutes or until vermicelli is golden.

2. Add water, chicken, shrimp, peas, roasted red pepper and seasoning packet; bring to a boil.

3. Reduce heat to low. Cover; cook 12 to 15 minutes or until rice is tender, stirring occasionally.   *Makes 6 servings*

Turkey and Mushroom Wild Rice Casserole

2 tablespoons butter
1 cup sliced fresh mushrooms *or* 1 can (4 ounces) sliced mushrooms
1 small onion, chopped
1 stalk celery, chopped
2 cups diced cooked turkey breast
1 can (about 10¾ ounces) condensed cream of mushroom soup, undiluted
1 pouch (about 9 ounces) ready-to-serve wild rice
1 cup milk
2 tablespoons minced fresh chives
¼ teaspoon black pepper
½ cup chopped pecans

1. Preheat oven to 350°F.

2. Melt butter in large nonstick skillet over medium heat. Add mushrooms, onion and celery; cook and stir 5 minutes or until onion is translucent. Stir in turkey, soup, wild rice, milk, chives and pepper; mix well.

3. Spoon mixture into 2-quart baking dish. Sprinkle with pecans. Bake 15 to 18 minutes or until hot and bubbly.   *Makes 4 servings*

Chicken with Rice & Asparagus Pilaf

4 boneless skinless chicken breasts
3 teaspoons poultry seasoning, divided
2 tablespoons olive oil
1 medium onion, chopped
1 cup uncooked rice
1 clove garlic, minced
2 cups chicken broth
¾ teaspoon salt
1 pound asparagus, trimmed and cut into 2-inch pieces (about 3 cups)

1. Sprinkle each chicken breast with ¼ teaspoon poultry seasoning. Heat oil in large skillet over medium-high heat. Cook chicken about 2 minutes on each side. Remove from skillet.

2. Cook and stir onion in same skillet 3 minutes. Add rice and garlic; cook and stir 1 to 2 minutes. Add broth, remaining 2 teaspoons poultry seasoning and salt. Bring to a boil over high heat. Reduce heat to low; cook, covered, 5 minutes.

3. Stir in asparagus and chicken. Cook, covered, 10 to 12 minutes or until rice is tender and chicken is no longer pink in center.

Makes 4 servings

Chicken Florentine in Minutes

3 cups water
1 cup milk
2 tablespoons butter
2 packages (about 4 ounces each) fettuccine Alfredo or stroganoff
   pasta mix
4 cups fresh baby spinach, coarsely chopped
¼ teaspoon black pepper
1 package (about 10 ounces) refrigerated fully cooked chicken breast
   strips, cut into ½-inch pieces
¼ cup diced roasted red pepper
¼ cup sour cream

1. Bring water, milk and butter to a boil in large saucepan over medium-high heat. Stir in pasta mix, spinach and black pepper.

2. Reduce heat to medium. Cook and stir 8 minutes or until pasta is tender.

3. Stir in chicken and red pepper; cook 2 minutes or until heated through. Remove from heat. Stir in sour cream.   *Makes 4 servings*

Chicken Pot Pie with Onion Biscuits

1 package (1.8 ounces) classic white sauce mix
2¾ cups milk, divided
¼ teaspoon dried thyme leaves
1 package (10 ounces) frozen peas and carrots, thawed
1 package (10 ounces) roasted carved chicken breast, cut into bite-size pieces
1 cup all-purpose baking mix
1⅓ cups *French's*® French Fried Onions, divided
½ cup (2 ounces) shredded Cheddar cheese

1. Preheat oven to 400°F. Prepare white sauce mix according to package directions with 2¼ cups milk; stir in thyme. Mix vegetables, chicken and prepared white sauce in shallow 2-quart casserole.

2. Combine baking mix, ⅔ *cup* French Fried Onions and remaining ½ cup milk in medium bowl until blended. Drop 6 to 8 spoonfuls of dough over chicken mixture.

3. Bake 25 minutes or until biscuits are golden. Sprinkle biscuits with cheese and remaining ⅔ *cup* onions. Bake 3 minutes or until cheese is melted and onions are golden.   *Makes 6 servings*

Variation: For added Cheddar flavor, substitute *French's*® Cheddar French Fried Onions for the original flavor.

Prep Time: 15 minutes • Cook Time: 33 minutes

Tomato and Turkey Soup with Pesto

1 cup uncooked rotini pasta
1 can (10¾ ounces) condensed tomato soup, undiluted
2 cups (8 ounces) frozen Italian-style vegetables
1 cup milk
2 tablespoons prepared pesto
1 cup coarsely chopped cooked skinless turkey
2 tablespoons grated Parmesan cheese

1. Cook pasta according to package directions; drain. Set aside.

2. Meanwhile, combine soup, vegetables, milk and pesto in medium saucepan. Bring to a boil over medium heat; reduce heat to low. Simmer, partially covered, 10 minutes or until vegetables are tender.

3. Add pasta and turkey. Cook 3 minutes or until heated through. Sprinkle with cheese just before serving.   *Makes 4 servings*

15-Minute Chicken and Broccoli Risotto

1 tablespoon vegetable oil
1 small onion, chopped
2 packages (about 9 ounces each) ready-to-serve yellow rice
2 cups frozen chopped broccoli
1 package (about 6 ounces) refrigerated fully cooked chicken breast
   strips, cut into pieces
½ cup chicken broth or water
   Sliced almonds (optional)

1. Heat oil in large skillet over medium-high heat. Add onion; cook and stir 3 minutes or until translucent.

2. Knead rice in bag. Add rice, broccoli, chicken and broth to skillet. Cover; cook 6 to 8 minutes or until heated through, stirring occasionally. Garnish with almonds.   *Makes 4 servings*

Turkey and Biscuits

2 cans (10¾ ounces each)
   condensed cream of chicken
   soup
¼ cup dry white wine
¼ teaspoon poultry seasoning
2 packages (8 ounces each) frozen
   chopped asparagus, thawed
3 cups cubed cooked turkey
   Paprika (optional)
1 can (11 ounces) refrigerated
   flaky biscuit dough

1. Preheat oven to 350°F. Spray 13×9-inch baking dish with nonstick cooking spray.

2. Combine soup, wine and poultry seasoning in medium bowl. Arrange asparagus in single layer in prepared dish. Place turkey evenly over asparagus. Spread soup mixture over turkey. Sprinkle lightly with paprika, if desired.

3. Cover tightly with foil and bake 20 minutes. Remove from oven. *Increase oven temperature to 425°F.* Top with biscuit dough and bake, uncovered, 8 to 10 minutes or until biscuits are golden brown.

Makes 6 servings

Mexicali Chicken Stew

1 package (about 1 ounce) taco
　　seasoning mix, divided
12 ounces boneless skinless
　　chicken thighs*
　　Nonstick cooking spray
2 cans (about 14 ounces each)
　　stewed tomatoes with
　　onions, celery and green
　　peppers
1 package (10 ounces) frozen
　　corn
1 package (9 ounces) frozen
　　green beans
4 cups tortilla chips

*You may substitute boneless skinless
chicken breasts.*

1. Place half of taco seasoning in
small bowl. Cut chicken thighs
into 1-inch pieces; coat with taco seasoning.

2. Spray large nonstick skillet with cooking spray. Cook and stir
chicken 5 minutes over medium heat or until cooked through.
Add tomatoes, corn, green beans and remaining taco seasoning;
bring to a boil.

3. Reduce heat to medium-low; simmer 10 minutes. Serve with
tortilla chips.   *Makes 4 servings*

Serving Suggestion: Serve nachos with the stew. Spread tortilla
chips on a plate; dot with salsa and sprinkle with cheese.
Microwave on HIGH about 30 seconds or just until the cheese is
melted.

Prep and Cook Time: 20 minutes

Asian Noodles with Vegetables and Chicken

1 tablespoon vegetable oil
2 cups sliced shiitake or button mushrooms
2 cups snow peas, sliced diagonally in half
2 packages (1.6 ounces each) garlic and vegetable instant rice noodle soup mix
2 cups boiling water
2 packages (about 6 ounces each) refrigerated fully cooked chicken breast strips, cut into pieces
¼ teaspoon red pepper flakes
2 tablespoons lime juice
1 tablespoon soy sauce

1. Heat oil in large skillet over medium-high heat. Add mushrooms and snow peas; cook 2 to 3 minutes or until snow peas are crisp-tender. Remove from skillet.

2. Break up noodles from soup mixes. Combine noodles, 1 seasoning packet (reserve remaining seasoning packet for another use, if desired), water, chicken and red pepper flakes in skillet; mix well. Cook over medium-high heat 5 to 7 minutes or until liquid thickens.

3. Stir in reserved vegetables, lime juice and soy sauce.

Makes 4 servings

Mini Chicken Pot Pies

1 container (about 16 ounces) refrigerated reduced-fat
   buttermilk biscuits
1½ cups milk
1 package (1.8 ounces) white sauce mix
2 cups cut-up cooked chicken
1 cup frozen assorted vegetables, partially thawed
2 cups shredded Cheddar cheese
2 cups *French's*® French Fried Onions

1. Preheat oven to 400°F. Separate biscuits; press into 8 (8-ounce) custard cups, pressing up sides to form crust.

2. Whisk milk and sauce mix in medium saucepan. Bring to boiling over medium-high heat. Reduce heat to medium-low; simmer 1 minute, whisking constantly, until thickened. Stir in chicken and vegetables.

3. Spoon about ⅓ cup chicken mixture into each crust. Place cups on baking sheet. Bake 15 minutes or until golden brown. Top each with cheese and French Fried Onions. Bake 3 minutes or until golden. To serve, remove from cups and transfer to serving plates.

Makes 8 servings

Prep Time: 15 minutes • Cook Time: about 20 minutes

Artichoke-Olive Chicken Bake

1½ cups uncooked rotini pasta
1 tablespoon olive oil
1 medium onion, chopped
½ green bell pepper, chopped
2 cups shredded cooked chicken
1 can (about 14 ounces) diced tomatoes with Italian herbs
1 can (14 ounces) artichoke hearts, drained and quartered
1 can (6 ounces) sliced black olives, drained
1 teaspoon Italian seasoning
2 cups (8 ounces) shredded mozzarella cheese

1. Preheat oven to 350°F. Spray 2-quart casserole with nonstick cooking spray. Cook pasta according to package directions until al dente; drain.

2. Heat oil in large skillet over medium heat. Add onion and bell pepper; cook and stir 1 minute. Add pasta, chicken, tomatoes, artichokes, olives and Italian seasoning; mix until blended.

3. Place half of chicken mixture in prepared casserole; sprinkle with half of cheese. Top with remaining chicken mixture and cheese. Bake, covered, 35 minutes or until hot and bubbly.   *Makes 8 servings*

Zesty Turkey Pot Pie

1 tablespoon vegetable oil
1 small onion, finely chopped
1 jalapeño pepper,* seeded and minced
1 pound ground turkey
1 package (16 ounces) frozen mixed vegetables
½ teaspoon dried thyme
½ teaspoon black pepper
2 cans (10¾ ounces each) condensed golden mushroom soup, undiluted
1 package (11 ounces) refrigerated breadstick dough (12 breadsticks)

Jalapeño peppers can sting and irritate the skin, so wear rubber gloves when handling peppers and do not touch your eyes.

1. Preheat oven to 350°F. Grease 13×9-inch casserole. Heat oil in large skillet over medium heat. Add onion and jalapeño; cook and stir 5 minutes or until tender. Add turkey; cook, stirring to break up meat.

2. Stir in vegetables, thyme and black pepper. Cook 5 minutes or until vegetables are thawed. Stir in soup. Cook 5 to 10 minutes or until mixture is heated through. Spoon turkey mixture into prepared casserole.*

3. Pull and stretch breadsticks to lengthen, pressing ends together if necessary to reach across baking dish. Arrange breadsticks in lattice pattern over turkey mixture. Bake 15 to 20 minutes or until breadsticks are golden brown. *Makes 6 servings*

The turkey mixture must be hot when it is spooned into the casserole to prevent breadstick bottoms from becoming gummy.

Easy Chicken Chalupas

1 fully cooked roasted chicken (about 2 pounds)
8 flour tortillas
2 cups shredded Cheddar cheese
1 cup mild green chile salsa
1 cup mild red salsa

1. Preheat oven to 350°F. Spray 13×9-inch baking dish with nonstick cooking spray. Shred chicken; discard skin and bones.

2. Place 2 tortillas in bottom of prepared dish, overlapping slightly. Layer tortillas with 1 cup chicken, ½ cup cheese and ¼ cup of each salsa. Repeat layers.

3. Bake 25 minutes or until hot and bubbly.   *Makes 6 servings*

Serving Suggestions: Serve this easy main dish with some custom toppings on the side such as sour cream, chopped cilantro, sliced black olives, sliced green onions and sliced avocado.

Green Chile-Chicken Casserole

4 cups shredded cooked chicken
1½ cups green enchilada sauce
1 can (10¾ ounces) condensed cream of chicken soup, undiluted
1 container (8 ounces) sour cream
1 can (4 ounces) diced mild green chiles
½ cup vegetable oil
12 (6-inch) corn tortillas
1½ cups (6 ounces) shredded Colby-Jack cheese, divided

1. Preheat oven to 325°F. Grease 13×9-inch casserole. Combine chicken, enchilada sauce, soup, sour cream and chiles in large skillet. Cook and stir over medium-high heat until heated through.

2. Heat oil in separate deep skillet. Fry tortillas just until softened; drain on paper towels. Place 4 tortillas on bottom of prepared casserole. Layer with one third of chicken mixture and ½ cup cheese. Repeat layers twice.

3. Bake 15 to 20 minutes or until cheese is melted and casserole is hot and bubbly. *Makes 6 servings*

Variation: Shredded Mexican cheese blend can be substituted for the Colby-Jack cheese.

Simmered Tuscan Chicken

**2 tablespoons olive oil
1 pound boneless, skinless chicken breasts, cut into 1-inch cubes
2 cloves garlic, finely chopped
2 medium potatoes, cut into ½-inch cubes (about 4 cups)
1 medium red bell pepper, cut into large pieces
1 jar (1 pound 10 ounces) RAGÚ® Old World Style® Pasta Sauce
1 teaspoon dried basil leaves, crushed
  Salt and ground black pepper to taste**

1. In 12-inch skillet, heat olive oil over medium-high heat and cook chicken with garlic until chicken is thoroughly cooked. Remove chicken and set aside.

2. In same skillet, add potatoes and bell pepper. Cook over medium heat, stirring occasionally, 5 minutes. Stir in remaining ingredients. Bring to a boil over high heat. Reduce heat to low and simmer, covered, stirring occasionally, 35 minutes or until potatoes are tender. Return chicken to skillet and heat through. *Makes 6 servings*

Warm Chicken & Couscous Salad

1 tablespoon olive oil
12 ounces chicken tenders or boneless skinless chicken breasts,
    cut into strips
2 teaspoons Cajun or blackened seasoning
1 teaspoon minced garlic
2 cups frozen broccoli, carrot and red bell pepper blend
1 can (about 14 ounces) chicken broth
1 cup uncooked couscous
3 cups packed torn spinach leaves
¼ cup poppy seed dressing

1. Heat oil in large nonstick skillet over medium-high heat. Toss chicken with Cajun seasoning in medium bowl. Add chicken and garlic to skillet; cook and stir 3 minutes or until chicken is cooked through.

2. Add mixed vegetables and broth to skillet; bring to a boil. Stir in couscous. Remove from heat.

3. Cover and let stand 5 minutes. Stir in spinach; transfer to serving plates. Drizzle with dressing. *Makes 4 servings*

Serving Suggestion: This quick salad goes great with a side of fresh fruit.

Prep and Cook Time: 20 minutes

Meatless Meals

Vegetarian Jambalaya

- **1 tablespoon vegetable oil**
- **½ cup diced green or red bell pepper**
- **1 can (about 14 ounces) diced tomatoes with chiles**
- **1 package (12 ounces) ground taco/burrito flavor soy meat substitute, crumbled**
- **1 package (about 9 ounces) New Orleans style ready-to-serve jambalaya rice**
- **2 tablespoons water**

1. Heat oil in large skillet over medium-high heat. Add bell pepper; cook and stir 3 minutes.

2. Add tomatoes, soy crumbles and rice; mix well. Stir in water.

3. Cook 5 minutes, uncovered, or until heated through.

Makes 4 servings

Four-Cheese Mac & Cheese

1 package (16 ounces) uncooked elbow macaroni
4 cups milk
4 cups (16 ounces) shredded sharp Cheddar cheese
4 cups (16 ounces) shredded American cheese
2 cups (8 ounces) shredded Muenster cheese
2 cups (8 ounces) shredded mozzarella cheese
½ cup dried bread crumbs (optional)

1. Preheat oven to 350°F. Cook macaroni according to package directions. Drain; keep warm.

2. Bring milk to a simmer in large saucepan over medium heat. Reduce heat to low. Gradually add cheeses, stirring constantly. Cook and stir 5 minutes or until smooth.

3. Place macaroni in 4-quart casserole or individual ovenproof dishes. Pour cheese sauce over pasta and stir until well blended. Sprinkle with bread crumbs, if desired. Bake 50 to 60 minutes or until hot and bubbly.

Makes 8 servings

Mexican-Style Rice and Cheese

1 can (about 15 ounces) Mexican-style beans
1 can (about 14 ounces) diced tomatoes with jalapeños
2 cups (8 ounces) shredded Monterey Jack or Colby cheese, divided
1½ cups uncooked converted long-grain rice
1 large onion, finely chopped
½ (8-ounce) package cream cheese
3 cloves garlic, minced

SLOW COOKER DIRECTIONS

1. Spray inside of slow cooker with nonstick cooking spray. Combine beans, tomatoes, 1 cup cheese, rice, onion, cream cheese and garlic in slow cooker; mix well.

2. Cover; cook on LOW 6 to 8 hours.

3. Sprinkle with remaining 1 cup cheese just before serving.

Makes 6 to 8 servings

Prep Time: 10 minutes • Cook Time: 6 to 8 hours (LOW)

Baked Tomato Risotto

1 jar (28 ounces) pasta sauce
1 can (about 14 ounces) vegetable broth
2 cups sliced zucchini
1 cup arborio rice
1 can (4 ounces) sliced mushrooms, drained
2 cups (8 ounces) shredded mozzarella cheese

1. Preheat oven to 350°F. Spray 3-quart casserole with nonstick cooking spray.

2. Combine pasta sauce, broth, zucchini, rice and mushrooms in prepared casserole.

3. Bake, covered, 30 minutes. Remove from oven; stir. Cover; bake 15 to 20 minutes or until rice is tender. Remove from oven; sprinkle evenly with cheese. Bake, uncovered, 5 minutes or until cheese is melted.

Makes 6 servings

Vegetarian Asian Noodles with Peanut Sauce

½ package (about 9 ounces) uncooked udon noodles* *or* 4 ounces
    uncooked whole wheat spaghetti
1 tablespoon vegetable oil
2 cups snow peas, cut diagonally into bite-size pieces
1 cup shredded carrots
¼ cup hot water
¼ cup peanut butter
¼ cup chopped green onions
2 to 4 tablespoons hot chili sauce with garlic
1 tablespoon soy sauce
¼ cup dry-roasted peanuts

Udon noodles, wheat flour noodles, are usually available in the Asian section of natural food stores or large supermarkets.

1. Cook noodles according to package directions. Drain; keep warm.

2. Heat oil in large skillet over medium-high heat. Add snow peas and carrots; stir-fry 2 minutes. Remove from heat.

3. Add water, peanut butter, green onions, chili sauce and soy sauce to skillet; mix well. Stir in noodles; toss well to coat. Sprinkle with peanuts. Serve warm or at room temperature. *Makes 4 servings*

Tip: To save time, use packaged shredded carrots.

Fiesta Broccoli, Rice and Beans

2 cups frozen broccoli florets
2 tablespoons water
2 cups uncooked instant rice
½ teaspoon chili powder
1 can (about 15 ounces) black beans, rinsed and drained
1 cup salsa or picante sauce
¼ cup (1 ounce) shredded Cheddar or pepper jack cheese

1. Place broccoli and water in medium microwavable dish. Cover loosely with plastic wrap; cook on HIGH 4 to 5 minutes or until crisp-tender.

2. Cook rice according to package directions, adding chili powder to cooking water.

3. Stir beans and salsa into hot cooked rice. Top each serving of rice and beans with broccoli and cheese. *Makes 4 servings*

Prep and Cook Time: 20 minutes

Bowtie Zucchini

¼ cup vegetable oil
1 cup chopped onion
2 cloves garlic, minced
5 small zucchini, cut into thin strips
⅔ cup whipping cream
1 package (16 ounces) bowtie pasta, cooked and drained
3 tablespoons grated Parmesan cheese
Salt and black pepper

1. Preheat oven to 350°F.

2. Heat oil in large skillet over medium-high heat. Add onion and garlic; cook and stir until onion is translucent. Add zucchini; cook and stir until tender.

3. Add cream; cook and stir until thickened. Add pasta and cheese to skillet. Season with salt and pepper. Transfer mixture to 2-quart casserole. Cover and bake 15 minutes or until heated through.

Makes 8 servings

Cheese & Chile Enchiladas

1 package (8 ounces) cream cheese, softened
2 cups (8 ounces) shredded Cheddar cheese, divided
1 can (4 ounces) diced mild green chiles, drained
¼ cup sliced green onions
6 (6-inch) flour tortillas
1 cup chunky salsa

1. Preheat oven to 350°F. Lightly spray 11×7-inch baking dish with nonstick cooking spray.

2. Beat cream cheese in medium bowl with electric mixer at medium speed until smooth. Add 1 cup Cheddar cheese, chiles and green onions; beat until blended.

3. Spread ¼ cup cream cheese mixture down center of each tortilla; roll up. Place, seam-side down, in prepared baking dish. Pour salsa over tortillas. Sprinkle with remaining 1 cup Cheddar cheese; cover. Bake 20 to 25 minutes or until heated through. *Makes 6 servings*

Prep Time: 15 minutes • Bake Time: 25 minutes

Pesto & Tortellini Soup

1 package (9 ounces) fresh cheese tortellini
3 cans (about 14 ounces each) vegetable broth
1 jar (7 ounces) roasted red peppers, drained and thinly sliced
¾ cup frozen green peas
3 to 4 cups packed stemmed fresh spinach
1 to 2 tablespoons pesto
   Grated Parmesan cheese (optional)

1. Cook tortellini according to package directions; drain.

2. Meanwhile, bring broth to a boil in large saucepan over high heat. Add cooked tortellini, peppers and peas; return to a boil. Reduce heat to medium and simmer 1 minute.

3. Remove from heat; stir in spinach and pesto. Garnish with Parmesan.

Makes 6 servings

Note: To easily remove stems from spinach leaves, fold each leaf in half, then pull stem toward top of leaf. Discard stems.

Prep and Cook Time: 14 minutes

Three Cheese Baked Ziti

1 container (15 ounces) part-skim ricotta cheese
2 eggs, beaten
¼ cup grated Parmesan cheese
1 box (16 ounces) ziti pasta, cooked and drained
1 jar (1 pound 10 ounces) RAGÚ® Chunky Pasta Sauce
1 cup shredded mozzarella cheese (about 4 ounces)

1. Preheat oven to 350°F. In large bowl, combine ricotta cheese, eggs and Parmesan cheese; set aside.

2. In another bowl, thoroughly combine pasta and Ragú Pasta Sauce.

3. In 13×9-inch baking dish, spoon ½ of the pasta mixture; evenly top with ricotta cheese mixture, then remaining pasta mixture. Sprinkle with mozzarella cheese. Bake 30 minutes or until heated through. Serve, if desired, with additional heated pasta sauce. *Makes 8 servings*

Prep: 20 minutes • Cook: 30 minutes

Parmesan Bean Casserole

2 tablespoons olive oil
1 cup chopped onion
2 teaspoons minced garlic
1 teaspoon dried oregano
¼ teaspoon black pepper
2 cans (about 14 ounces each) diced tomatoes with onion and garlic
1 jar (about 14 ounces) roasted red peppers, drained and cut into ½-inch pieces
2 cans (about 15 ounces each) Great Northern beans, rinsed and drained
¾ cup shredded Parmesan cheese
1 tablespoon chopped fresh basil *or* 1 teaspoon dried basil

1. Heat oil in large saucepan over medium heat. Add onion, garlic, oregano and black pepper; cook and stir 5 minutes or until onion is translucent.

2. Increase heat to high. Add tomatoes and red peppers; cover and bring to a boil.

3. Reduce heat to medium. Stir in beans; cover and simmer 5 minutes, stirring occasionally. Stir in cheese and basil. *Makes 6 servings*

Prep and Cook Time: 20 minutes

Acknowledgments

The publisher would like to thank the companies
listed below for the use of their recipes and photographs
in this publication.

Reckitt Benckiser Inc.

Unilever

METRIC CONVERSION CHART

VOLUME MEASUREMENTS (dry)

1/8 teaspoon = 0.5 mL
1/4 teaspoon = 1 mL
1/2 teaspoon = 2 mL
3/4 teaspoon = 4 mL
1 teaspoon = 5 mL
1 tablespoon = 15 mL
2 tablespoons = 30 mL
1/4 cup = 60 mL
1/3 cup = 75 mL
1/2 cup = 125 mL
2/3 cup = 150 mL
3/4 cup = 175 mL
1 cup = 250 mL
2 cups = 1 pint = 500 mL
3 cups = 750 mL
4 cups = 1 quart = 1 L

VOLUME MEASUREMENTS (fluid)

1 fluid ounce (2 tablespoons) = 30 mL
4 fluid ounces (1/2 cup) = 125 mL
8 fluid ounces (1 cup) = 250 mL
12 fluid ounces (1 1/2 cups) = 375 mL
16 fluid ounces (2 cups) = 500 mL

WEIGHTS (mass)

1/2 ounce = 15 g
1 ounce = 30 g
3 ounces = 90 g
4 ounces = 120 g
8 ounces = 225 g
10 ounces = 285 g
12 ounces = 360 g
16 ounces = 1 pound = 450 g

DIMENSIONS

1/16 inch = 2 mm
1/8 inch = 3 mm
1/4 inch = 6 mm
1/2 inch = 1.5 cm
3/4 inch = 2 cm
1 inch = 2.5 cm

OVEN TEMPERATURES

250°F = 120°C
275°F = 140°C
300°F = 150°C
325°F = 160°C
350°F = 180°C
375°F = 190°C
400°F = 200°C
425°F = 220°C
450°F = 230°C

BAKING PAN SIZES

Utensil	Size in Inches/Quarts	Metric Volume	Size in Centimeters
Baking or Cake Pan (square or rectangular)	8 × 8 × 2	2 L	20 × 20 × 5
	9 × 9 × 2	2.5 L	23 × 23 × 5
	12 × 8 × 2	3 L	30 × 20 × 5
	13 × 9 × 2	3.5 L	33 × 23 × 5
Loaf Pan	8 × 4 × 3	1.5 L	20 × 10 × 7
	9 × 5 × 3	2 L	23 × 13 × 7
Round Layer Cake Pan	8 × 1 1/2	1.2 L	20 × 4
	9 × 1 1/2	1.5 L	23 × 4
Pie Plate	8 × 1 1/4	750 mL	20 × 3
	9 × 1 1/4	1 L	23 × 3
Baking Dish or Casserole	1 quart	1 L	—
	1 1/2 quart	1.5 L	—
	2 quart	2 L	—